Dear Parent:

Do you want to spark your child's creativity? Do you want your child to become a confident writer? Road to Writing can help.

Road to Writing is a unique creative writing program that gives even the youngest writers a chance to express themselves. Featuring five distinct levels, or Miles, the Road to Writing program accompanies children from their first attempts at writing to comfortably writing on their own.

A Creative Start
For children who "write" stories by drawing pictures
• easy picture prompts • familiar subjects • places to draw

Creative Writing With Help
For children who write easy words with help
• detailed picture prompts • places to draw and label

Creative Writing On Your Own
For children who write simple sentences on their own
• basic story starters • popular topics • places to write

First Journals
For children who are comfortable writing short paragraphs
• more complex story starters • space for free writing

Journals
For children who want to try different kinds of writing
• cues for poems, jokes, stories • brainstorming pages

There's no need to hurry through the Miles. Road to Writing is designed without age or grade levels. Children can progress at their own speed, developing confidence and pride in their writing ability along the way.

Road to Writing—"write" from the start!

Look for these
Road to Writing
books

Mile 1

Animal Crackers
Cool School
Super Me!

Mile 2

Boo!
Get A Clue!
Road Trip

Mile 3

Happily Never After: Tangled Tales
Monkey Business
Sports Shorts

Tips for Using this Book

- Read each page aloud to your child. Then let your child draw a response—right in the book!

- Don't worry—there are no "right" or "wrong" answers. This book is a place for your child to be creative.

- If your child wants to skip ahead, that's fine. It's okay to jump from page to page.

- Remember to encourage your child with lots of praise.

Pencils, pens, and crayons are all suitable for use in this book. Markers are not recommended.

A GOLDEN BOOK • New York
Golden Books Publishing Company, Inc. New York, New York 10106

ISBN: 0-307-45401-0   R MM

Cool School

by Sarah Albee and

by sydney

(your name)

illustrated by
Lynne Cravath and

illustrated

(your name)

What does your school look like?

Draw it.

How do you get to school?
Draw a picture that shows how.

How does this Martian get to school?

Draw a picture that shows how.

Draw a picture of
your favorite teacher.

Draw what you think your teacher looked like as a kid your age.

Dress up these words so they *look* like what they *mean*.

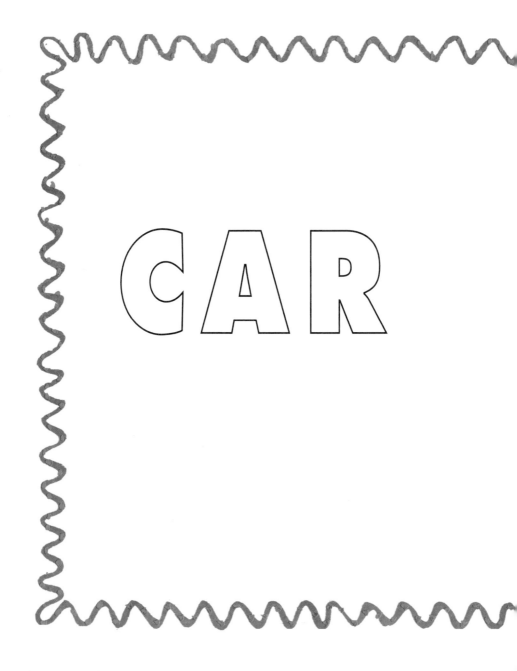

Draw the perfect outfit
for the first day
of school.

Draw the perfect costume for Halloween.

Nice costume!

Your class pet grew
A HUNDRED TIMES BIGGER
overnight!

Draw what it looks like.

What could these people bring for show and tell?

Draw your ideas.

Draw you and your friends on the playground at school.

Lunchtime!

Design your own
lunch box.

What's for lunch?
Draw it.

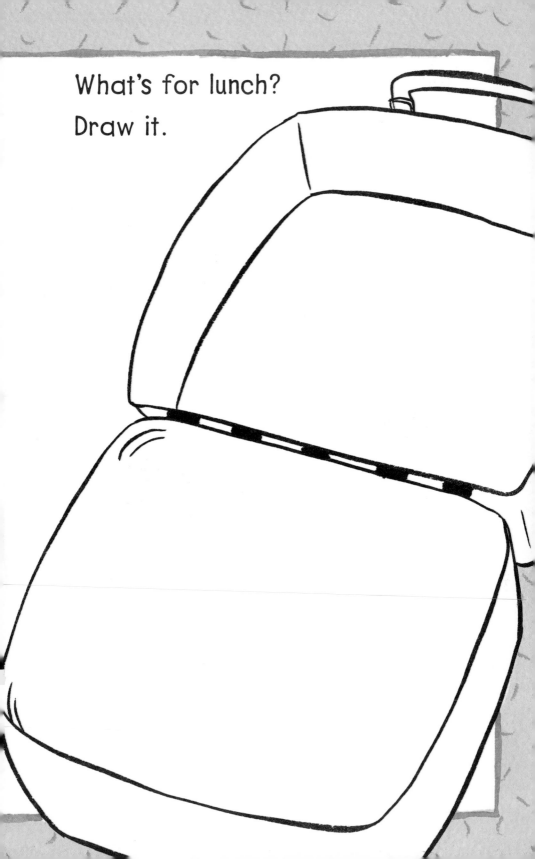

You're the teacher for a day!
What will you teach?

Pick one of these subjects
or make up your own.

how to make
a funny face

how to stand
on your head

how to make
an ice cream sundae

how to _____

Draw yourself teaching the class.

Dress up these words so they *look* like what they *mean.*

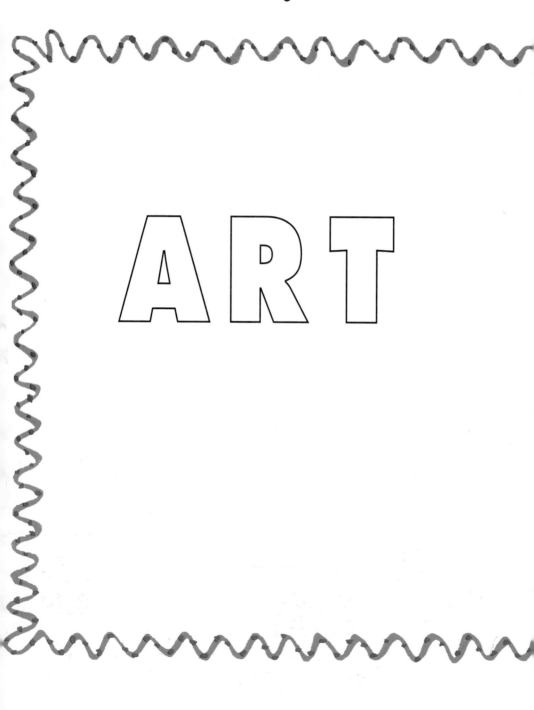

LUNCH

GYM

It's job day at school.
Draw what you would
wear if you were a:

doctor

basketball player

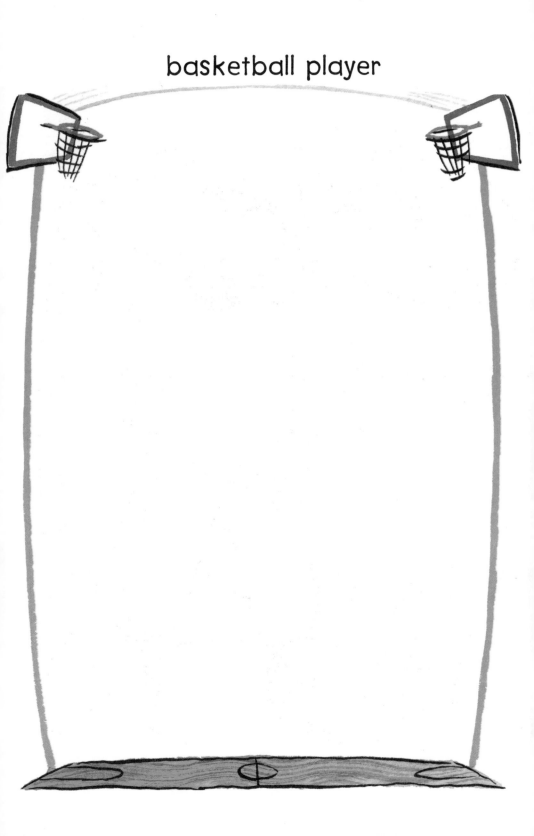

HOMEWORK

Name **PEGLEG PETE**

Draw three things that have whiskers.

Draw a cool pair of sneakers for gym class.

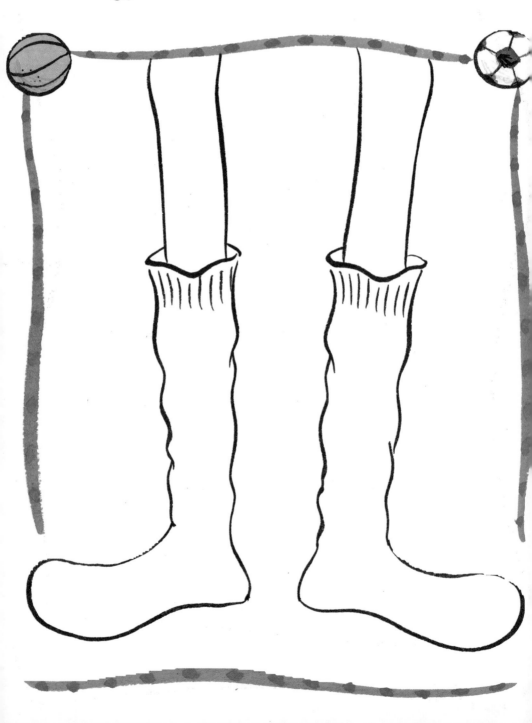

Draw yourself playing your favorite sport.

Snow day!

Draw what you and your friends will do instead of going to school.

Think about the best book you ever read in class.

Draw a picture of you with your favorite character from the book.

Draw three things you did in school today.

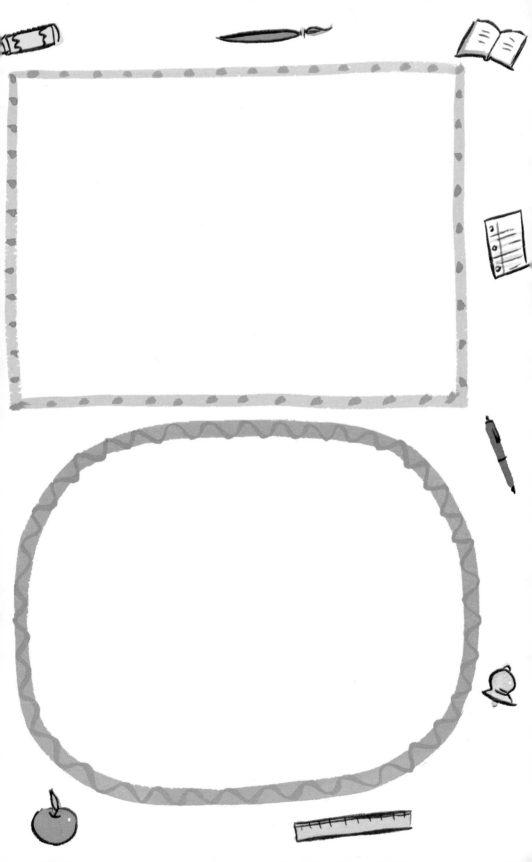

Draw three things you'd like to do in school tomorrow.

Yikes!
A *dinosaur* followed you home
from school!

Draw it.

HOMEWORK

Name *Wendy Wart*

Draw three things that can fly.

It's Class Picture Day!
Draw your class.
Put yourself in the front row.

Draw what you think you will look like next year.